From the Author:

A dedication and other notes about this curriculum

*Dedicated to Waylon, Tucker and Hank who are the reason **why this curriculum exists.***

I am the proud mother of three boys, ages ranging from three to seven-years-old. I coordinate the VBS and Religious Education for my small town church and I also homeschool our children. Our family lives in a quaint little house in the woods, and let's just say we're a little "outdoorsy". Most of our days consist of warm cups of coffee, hiking, foraging, building forts, cutting firewood and just getting downright dirty. I'm afraid to admit to the amount of dirt and mud that finds its way into my home on a regular basis.

Now you can imagine what might have inspired me to write this curriculum. In teaching my own children, I quickly realized how easily nature resonates with them, and they are regularly marveling at God's beautiful creation.

At the same time, my church is rather small and has a smaller budget to work with. Having planned VBS in the past, I know how difficult it can be to *afford* it. Of course the bigger curriculums are lovely, but after purchasing the curriculum plus all the supplies, my budget would be very quickly blown. Despite our church's size, it tends to pack a big punch in the VBS department, so I really want to be able to deliver.

Alas, I had the idea to write this curriculum. Not just because I wanted to save some money, but because my own children inspired this vision that I could not wait to spark into existence. When it came time for us to host VBS, it was a total hit. Even the older kids loved it and their attendance numbers multiplied every day.

I have my children, husband, and my parish community to thank for being able to create this curriculum to share with others now.

Much love and blessings to you all,

Jena Robertson

OTHER THINGS TO KNOW ABOUT THIS CURRICULUM:

What this curriculum includes:

- Daily lesson plans for three essential stations

- Script for camp opening and closing

- Schedule blank copy sheets

- A suggestive supplies shopping list

- Interactive and in depth Bible lessons throughout

- Emphasis on the story of Job

- Emphasis on real-life wilderness survival safety and situations

- Inclusion of the Holy Trinity

This program is geared towards ages K-8, however, it can easily be adapted to include teens.

What this curriculum does *not* include is:

- Additional supplies nor the accessibility to any specific supplies

- Theme specific music

- Videos or screens of any kind (unless you choose to use YouTube on a big screen for music)

If you've planned VBS before, you will know that you purchase the curriculum and then you buy daily activities, crafts and trinkets from that company as well. That is not the case with this curriculum, as I do not have the capacity to offer this—nor is it necessary for this theme. You will find that this curriculum is very nature-oriented and generally follows the Montessori-style of learning. All of the keepsakes will be handmade. A shopping list of craft supplies will be provided.

There *is* music! You'll just have to source the music yourself and there is no "theme" song. Music will be at the VBS coordinator's discretion—YouTube, live music, downloads, CD, cassette player—haha? Whatever works. Don't overthink the music. I'll get back to that shortly.

As for the TV's and screens, we're "lost in the woods" here, and there will be no screens!

**It is important to note that the table of contents is located at the back of this book.

Lost in the Woods
God leads the way!

At a glance:

This VBS program will teach children valuable Bible stories and virtues, while also connecting them to a huge part of God's beautiful creation—the woods! As a group of young and aspiring explorers, we will become "lost" in the wilderness. We will spend a week here and embark on several adventures. We will meet a hermit, learn real-life survival skills, explore Bible stories and science, and ultimately find a way to let "God Lead the Way" in our hearts.

Three essential stations:

Surviving the Woods: Each night, a different station leader(s) will present an essential survival skill. The groups will play out certain situations such as building a survival shelter/camp, filtering dirty water, etc. The general theme of this station is to encourage children to marvel at God's creation and understand that he filled the earth with various things to help us thrive—even when we are lost.

Bible Adventures: A station leader will read a Bible story (mostly from the book of Job) and relate it to a science demonstration or craft. At this station, we encourage kids to admire God's creation as well as reflect on the beloved Bible scriptures and stories.

Woodland Games: Games will take place outdoors, weather permitting. Here, we will play woodland and survival-themed games. The games will tie the Bible stories and our daily adventures all together in a fun and engaging way.

A glance at our daily schedule

4:40-5:00 PM: Students arrive and sign-in

5:00-5:15 PM: Introduction and Camp Opening

5:20-5:45 PM: 1st station

5:50-6:15 PM: 2nd station

6:20-6:50 PM: Dinner

6:55-7:20 PM: 3rd station

7:25-7:55 PM: Camp Closing

GROUPS:

- Preschool-Kindergarten

- 1-3rd grade

- 4-5th grade

- CREW LEADERS (helpers)

Notes:

- Groups will rotate the order of stations each night

Daily Schedule Blank Template

First, make five copies of the next page. (This template is an EXAMPLE). Once you've made five copies, write in your daily schedule on the separate days. Then, make copies in bulk to pass out!

DAILY SCHEDULE EXAMPLE

Station	Lil' Hooties	Wolf Pack	Bears
Camp Opening 5-5:15	ALL	ALL	ALL
1st station 5:20-5:45	Surviving the Wild	Woodland Games	Bible Adventures
2nd station 5:50-6:15	Woodland Games	Bible Adventures	Surviving the Wild
Meal/Snack 6:20-6:50	ALL	ALL	ALL
3rd Station 6:55-7:20	Bible Adventures	Surviving the Wild	Woodland Games
Camp Closing 7:25-7:55	ALL	ALL	ALL

I encourage you to alternate your group schedule daily. For example, the first day Lil' Hooties might go to Surviving the Woods first, but the next day it might be Woodland Games.

If you plan to alternate, it is important to label your schedule sheet with the date and make copies of it to give to your crew leaders each day.

You will also notice we have **three** groups. If you need more groups, make more copies and use different group names. If you do this, you will need to duplicate your stations accordingly.

DAILY SCHEDULE DATE: _____

Station	Lil' Hooties	Wolf Pack	Bears
Camp Opening	ALL	ALL	ALL
1st station			
2nd station			
Meal/Snack	ALL	ALL	ALL
3rd Station			
Camp Closing	ALL	ALL	ALL

FOR THE MUSIC COORDINATOR:

Note: Music can take place briefly at camp opening (time permitting), but most music will be done at Camp Closing after the Rowdy Woods skits.

1. Choose your music!

Music can be selected by the VBS Music Coordinator. Thanks to YouTube and other tech-y apps, music is not hard to obtain. I recommend choosing five or six songs that the students practice every day. Take care to choose appropriate Christian youth music. We find that kids really enjoy upbeat songs, but one or two slower ballads may be well-received as well.

2. Play the music!

Play them as you prefer (respecting your local copyright regulations, of course). For the record, when my church did this, we used a mixture of live and recorded music. As it happened for us, Rowdy Woods' character was musical. The kids *really* enjoyed singing with him. However, if your Rowdy is not musical, that's totally okay and not a requirement for the role.

3. Get into the music!

Go all in! Show the children that music is a fun way to worship together. If you're only half-way into it, the kids will notice and they'll reflect your awkward mood. You set the tone for the whole evening with the music, so shake your sillies out (never mind what the other adults in the room are thinking) and just have fun.

4. Dance to the music!

You may need to get creative and come up with your own moves. They need not be complicated. You will find that YouTube has some choreographed videos for Christian kids' music as well.

VBS SNACKS AND FOOD

You will notice that my examples all show as serving dinner. You will need to adjust this according to your own VBS schedule and preferences. Many churches do not offer a full meal at VBS, and that's okay. If you choose not to do a full meal and opt for a snack instead, you may want to shave off fifteen or so minutes from the allotted meal time in the example schedule.

Make your food situation easier by doing these things:

The first thing I recommend doing is appointing a trustworthy **meal time coordinator**. You have enough on your plate, let someone else take the meal (no pun intended). They will be in charge of enlisting the kitchen help, arranging the meal schedule and menu, and helping prepare the food. Below are recommendations for the meal time coordinator:

1. **Obtain an estimate for how many students are in attendance**

2. **Create food donation slips, dividing quantities of items as needed**

3. **Have a table set up before or after service over the course of a few Sundays and take sign ups for food donations. (Do this a few weeks prior to VBS)**

4. **You will need to document your donors and daily menu.**

5. **The donation slips will go with the donors as their informational sheet.**

6. **Be sure to take contact information for your donors, and send them reminders at least 48 hours in advance.**

The donors will be responsible for bringing the food as planned. Some may prepare it, or you may have assigned cooks prepare it in the kitchen.

Allergies: Any food allergies should be listed on students' registration forms and the VBS coordinator can provide a list of food allergies to the kitchen help at the start of the week. If a child has an allergy, take care to prepare their plate away from others. You can also suggest that the student brings their own snacks or meal.

*Some allergies to be especially aware of are peanuts and shellfish, as they induce anaphylaxis, which can be fatal.

At a Glance

DAY 1

Phrase of the day: "Even when we are lost..." (God leads the way!)

Mascot: Hootie the Owl: Hootie is an adorable hoot owl who has an amazing gift for finding its way around the woods.

At the beginning of the night (following the script) we will start with a daily devotional, meet our mascot of the night, and follow with songs and movement. We will then become lost. The coordinator will discharge them into their groups.

Key lessons for the day:

- The Book of Job

- Provision of the forest

- Using God's signs in nature, we learn about the science of telling direction.

- Lean on God when we feel lost in life

Quick summary of the stations:

- **Bible Adventures:** Read from the book of Job and do craft and experiment. The craft will send them away with a compass.

- **Surviving the Wild**: The three survival necessities—food, water, shelter. They will illustrate this in a triangle and relate it to the Holy Trinity. Station leader will then lead the groups in building a shelter.

- **Woodland games**: How can they help others find them? The kids will separate in to groups and play a version of hide and seek, using different tactics to tip the seekers off. The goal is for the seeker to be able to find the hidden within fifteen seconds so both hiders and seeker will need to work together.

- **Camp gathering (closing)**: At the end of the night, we will meet Rowdy Woods, a hermit with a relatable backstory and in need of finding Jesus!

Day 2

Phrase of the day: "Even when we are anxious…" (God leads the way!)

Mascot: Jumpy the Rabbit- Jumpy is a very anxious rabbit! Rabbits like Jumpy are known as prey animals, and we will explore their behavioral traits that occur because of this. We also learn the amazing plan God has for rabbits!

Key lessons for the day:

- The story of Job

- Provision of the forest

- Using God's tools in nature, we will discover ways to find and create light

- Learn to follow the light of Jesus

Quick summary of the stations:

- **Bible Adventures:** Continue to read about the story of Job. Job's bright light of life seemed to go out, and he must have felt so anxious! But through it all, he was still able to see God's light. The activity will send them away with a glowing keepsake.

- **Surviving the Wild**: The station leader(s) will give them another example of using a trinity— but this time for building a *fire*. Oxygen, fuel, and heat..just like we need the Holy Trinity, fire needs these three things to thrive. (It is up to the volunteers as to whether they actually want to use real fire or pretend. Real fire will need to be used outdoors and with extra safety precautions.)

- **Woodland games**: *"Tug of war"* and *"Googly Eyed Obstacles*

- **Camp Closing**: When we go back to camp we see Rowdy Woods again, and learn that Rowdy is afraid of the dark. We tell Rowdy not to be anxious, because God leads the way!

Day 3

Phrase of the day: "Even when things get messy..." (God leads the way!)

Mascot: Bobby the Beaver- Bobby is an adorable critter..with one problem. He can make a really big mess! But why? And what role does he play in God's creation? We learn today!

Key lessons for the day:

- Continue with the story of Job

- Science of the forest and its waterways

- Using God's tools in nature, we learn to be resourceful

- Learn to follow the light of Jesus

Quick summary of the stations:

- **Bible Adventures:** Revisit the story of Job. Afterwards we will do a waterway experiment. Refer to the parable of the speck and the log and discuss how sometimes it's easy to look at others' messes and criticize them. But perhaps we don't understand their situation. Perhaps we have our *own* messes!

- **Surviving the Wild**: Today we will learn a couple different methods to filter water naturally. Using ingredients from items in the crew leaders bags, we will make a hand-made water filter. We will demonstrate the filter and show how it cleans water. We will discuss the importance of maintaining our trash and debris around camp and being mindful of things we put into God's amazing water system.

- **Woodland games**: *Water collection*: using sponges or water balls, kids will have relay races to see who can fill their tub with the most water. The second game will be a log limbo.

- **Camp Closing**: When we go back to camp and we see Rowdy Woods again, and he gets sprayed by a skunk! We have to remind him that when life gets messy…God leads the way!

Day 4

Phrase of the day: "Even when we are confused …" (God leads the way!)

Mascot: Skippy the Squirrel- Skippy is a funny little squirrel who loves devouring acorns and nuts. He survives winter by spending a lot of time during the summer and fall burying his treasures! He's kind of like a woodland pirate. He sometimes forgets where he buries his treasure! But he never goes hungry because God always provides for him!

Key lessons for the day:

- Finish with the story of Job

- Using God's tools in nature, we learn to ID different kinds of foods.

- Learn to call on God when we are wanting

Quick summary of the stations:

- **Bible Adventures:** Finish the story of Job. Reflect on his hardships and how he still continues to value the ultimate treasure, which is the Kingdom of Heaven.

- **Surviving the Wild**: Today the kids will learn about different hunting and gathering skills. Some activities include camouflaging themselves as hunters, learning some basic hunting tactics, and looking at fruits and plants of the woods. They will take home a dandelion tea sample to try at home.

- **Woodland games**: *Treasure Hunt*: using water or sand in a pool, blindfolded students will use their hands to find certain treasures.

    Hide the treasure: one student will ask yes or no questions to determine where the rest of the students hid their treasure.

Camp Closing: We go back to camp and we see Rowdy Woods again. He had a bad hunt and is now very hungry! We have to remind him that God will lead the way!

Day 5

Phrase of the day: "Even when we are surprised..." (God leads the way!)

Mascot: Amy the Ant- Amy is an interesting critter of the woods, and always stays busy! Instead of being afraid of things that are coming, she and her tribe get to work and prepare!

Key lessons for the day:

- Story of Jesus and the calming of the storm

- Preparing our hearts for Jesus

- Using God's signs in nature, we learn to predict impending weather

- Learn to listen to God's voice/pay attention to nature around you

Quick summary of the stations:

- **Bible stories and science:** Share the story of Jesus and the calming of the storm. Discuss how fishermen today prepare for storms. Make a cork boat craft.

- **Surviving the Wild**: Nature is a powerful part of God's voice. If we pay close attention, we may see God trying to talk to us through nature. Today we will explore ways to read the weather in nature as well as prepare for possible bad weather. This will involve experiments with pine cones.

- **Woodland games**: *Messy Balloon Pop:* kids will take turns popping balloons with surprising contents.

- **Camp Closing/Closing program**: On day five, times at the stations will be shortened and we will come back to Camp Closing for our entire closing program. (Regular dinner time will be omitted, and optional celebratory dinner can occur afterwards). We will share the adventures of our week and perform the songs we learned. We will also have another Rowdy Woods skit, where he has regained his confidence and has learned to listen to God's voice in nature once again.

Description of Volunteer Duties

Registration/check-in: this person will need to arrive by 4:30. They will sit at table and check students in each evening. They may need to pass out name tags or accept walk-in registrations. They will be the point of contact at the door so they will need to be familiar with the stations, their locations, and the daily schedule.

Food servers: Food servers will need to arrive early (plan accordingly to your schedule), assuming the scheduled meal will take no longer than an hour to fix. They will be responsible for preparing, setting up, serving and cleaning up the kitchen when finished.

Meal time Coordinator: This person will be in charge of coordinating the meals or snacks. This includes creating a menu, acquiring food donations, and seeing that the meals are prepared and served, and that the kitchen is cleaned adequately when finished.

Station Leaders: These volunteers will need to arrive by 5:00. They will follow daily lesson plans. We encourage station leaders to obtain a copy of their lesson plans in advance so that they can have a good understanding of their activities. *For this particular program, it is desired that the "Surviving the Woods" station has a different leader each night. This would be a great opportunity for the survivalists out there!

Station helpers: Each station should have at least one helper. This person can serve as an extra set of hands in preparation of the station, as well as helping kids participate in the station activity.

Crew Leaders: Each group needs at least two crew leaders. These will likely be middle and high school students. The crew leaders will need to arrive between 4:40-5:00. Remember that the younger children are looking up to these older students. Only students with good conduct, a positive attitude, and Godly virtues should be chosen for these roles.

Music: The music person will lead the kids in worship songs and teach them simple movements. The music will take place at the beginning and the end of the evenings during the campsite gatherings.

Personalities: Rowdy Woods is a primary character throughout the week. He will portray a stranded man-gone hermit. He is grouchy, but humorous as well. Throughout the week, he learns about Jesus and the kids help him along on his journey to faith. In the end, he grows to love Jesus and can finally see God's hand in everything he does.

The lead explorer (VBS coordinator) will begin the week by leading the group of "summer campers" into the forest only to come out completely lost. The leader will direct camp opening and closing every night.

DAILY PREPARATION:

• Have crew leader bags ready, and full of miscellaneous supplies. Everything from bandaids, empty toilet paper rolls, dryer lent, paper, string, fabric, etc. They will be asked to empty their bags at a station so they can brain storm how to use those things to survive.

• Have daily schedules completed and copied to pass out to all helpers.

Budget Example and Template
Fill in blanks as desired. Copies may be made if desired.

Items	Estimated budget	Actual expense	
Nightly Mascots (5)	$20-$50 each	$12.99 a piece	Fill in details of products if desired
Misc. decor			
Backdrop(s)			
Craft paper for decorations			
Misc. items, i.e.,crew leader bags, name tags, etc.			
Day 1 craft supplies (Bible Adventures)			
Day 2 craft supplies (Bible Adventures)			
Day 3 craft supplies (Bible Adventures)			
Day 4 craft supplies (Bible Adventures)			
Day 5 craft supplies (Bible Adventures)			
Meal or snacks	Ask for donations		

Items	Estimated budget	Actual expense

LET'S GO SHOPPING!

Your shopping list, organized by each station.

DAY 1:

BIBLE ADVENTURES

ITEM	SUGGESTED SHOPPING LOCATION	OTHER NOTES
Compass	Oriental Trading	
String for necklace		
Beads for decorating		
DAY 2		
Lantern Craft	Oriental Trading	
OR glow stick cross necklace	Oriental Trading	
Beads for decorating		
DAY 3		
Aluminum baking trays	Local grocery store	
Aluminum foil	Local grocery store	
Rocks, pebbles	Outside or craft store	
Sticks	Outside or craft store	
Water pitcher	Local grocery store	
DAY 4		
Wood slabs or pieces	Hobby Lobby or craft store	
Paint	Craft store	

ITEM	SUGGESTED SHOPPING LOCATION	OTHER NOTES
DAY 5		
Wine corks in bulk	Oriental trading	
Rubber bands	Local store	
Popsicle sticks	Craft store	
Foam paper, multi colors	Craft store	
Scissors	Local store or on hand	
Hot glue gun(s)	Craft store	
Hot glue sticks		

WOODLAND GAMES

Crepe paper	Party store	
Rocks	Outside or craft store	
Sticks		
Pieces of fabric	Craft store	
Hoola hoops (several)	Walmart or dollar store	
2-4 small pools	Walmart	
Sponges	Walmart	
Water balls	Walmart	
Pool noodles	Walmart	
Sand buckets	Walmart	
Googly eye goggles	Hobby Lobby or Amazon	

Sturdy string	Craft store
Balloons	Walmart or party store
Water balloons	
Colored powder	Amazon
Confetti	Party store
Toothpicks	
Clothespins	
Jump ropes	

SURVIVING THE WOODS

Miscellaneous items for crew leader bags		Any random assortment of items will do such as string, fabric, bandaids, anything
Pool noodles, optional for shelter		
Blanket or sheet, optional for shelter		
Logs and fire "kindle"		
Rocks for "fire ring"		
Emptied water bottles		
Cotton balls or coffee filters		
Charcoal		

Sand	Garden center
Pea gravel or pebbles	Craft store or garden center
Larger rocks	Craft store or garden center
Crew leader bags	Oriental Trading or Hobby Lobby
Scissors	
Toy bow and arrows with targets	Walmart or sports store
Nerf Rifles (and target)	Walmart or Target
Children's fishing poles	Walmart or sports store
Magnetic fishing game (for preschool/kinder)	Walmart or Target
For Friday's activity, refer to the lesson plan for a list of items needed. They can be used if need be.	

Also: Mascots for camp opening, which include an owl, rabbit, beaver, squirrel, and an ant. These can be drawn, printed, or purchased as stuffed animals.

BIBLE ADVENTURES DAY 1

Daily Affirmation: Even when we are lost…*God leads the way!*

Read to the children: Welcome to Bible Adventures! I know that you are lost in the woods, but I have great news. You have come to a really amazing place! This is where we take an adventure in our minds, to the time of the Bible!

If you are able to listen to my every word, I can send you away from here with a very special tool! Let's all gather around and listen.

The Story of Job

Read to the children: There once lived a man by the name of Job (Jobe). He lived in a land called "Uz". Can you say that? "Uz"! Very good. Job had an *awesome* life. He had wealth, a successful business , a healthy life and family, and most of all he loved God very much. When we love God, we show that by loving others and being kind. Job was very careful to never do evil and to always be fair and kind to all those who knew him. And God had blessed Job with all these wonderful things.

But Job's life began to take a turn one day after Satan decided to start tormenting him. Satan thought that Job would abandon God as soon as all his treasures were taken away. Satan had one goal. It was to tear a God-loving man away from his Father! Not a nice thing to do, huh? However, God did not think that Job would ever abandon Him. God was sure of this because He knew Job's heart. There is no one in this woods or on this earth who knows our hearts like God!

So Satan began to taunt Job and wreak havoc on his life. To "wreak havoc" means to really mess things up. One day, a messenger rushed to Job's home with tragic news.

The farmhand was frantic with fear and said, "Sir! Your oxen were plowing with the donkeys feeding beside them when the Sabeans raided us. They drove away the animals and killed all the farmhands except for me. I am the only one left!"

Job was very sad to hear that his farmhands had died. He had loved them as if they were his own family. Not to mention that their work was very important to the success of Job's business. Job felt *lost* and he wondered what he and his farmhands had done to deserve this terrible fate. Job did not know that he was in the middle of a battle between God and Satan—good and evil. He did not know that Satan, who was invisible to him, was behind this horrible thing. But nevertheless, Job still did not curse God and instead prayed to Him.

Discuss:

Ask the children:

1. Have you ever had to work on a project with other people? When we work on projects with other people, it helps us divide up our duties and make things easier and faster. So when all Job's farmhands died, how do you think that made it hard for Job to work the fields? And what would he do without them? Do you think he felt *lost?*

2. Sometimes we wonder why bad things happen to us. For example*, why* did we get lost in the woods today? (Allow kids to answer) We may not know the answer today.

Read: There is something very special about God that I want to tell you. Even when we are lost ("God leads the way!"). That's right! Staying close to God is like having a compass close to us at all times! And if we have a compass what do we know? (Directions!). That's right, a compass helps us understand where we are going.

Compass craft

Supplies needed: compass pieces, string, beads. (Or compass necklace kits from OT).

Offer a quick demonstration on how a compass works. Instruct the kids on how to make the compass craft. Enlist crew leaders and other adult helpers to ensure students understand. When everyone is finished, they may take the craft home.

If you purchased compass craft kits from Oriental Trading, assemble them according to the instructions that they came with. Otherwise, you will simply be stringing beads and compasses to make custom necklaces or bracelets.

Before students leave your station, be sure to thank them and remind them to keep their hearts on God, even on the bad days.

SURVIVING THE WOODS DAY 1

Daily affirmation: Even when we are lost…*God leads the way*!

The Holy Trinity of Survival

In this lesson the station leader(s) discuss the Holy Trinity and relate it to the "Holy Trinity of survival."

Read to the children: Welcome to Surviving the Woods! Wow, it has been quite a day, huh? We came out here to the wilderness to marvel at God's beautiful creation and we got lost! But that's okay, because we know that even when we are lost (God leads the way!).

Here, we are going to put our heads together and learn how to survive the woods. Come to think of it, surviving in the wild has a lot of similarities to surviving the great big journey of life as well. What I mean is that sometimes life throws us some curveballs, and we have to learn to use what we have to survive. To survive and thrive in life, we always need to lean on God. We pray to the Father, who is our creator, and the Son, who is our savior Jesus Christ, and the Holy Spirit, which is the part of God that is within us.

If we did not have the Father, we would not even exist!

If we did not have Jesus, we would not have access to eternal life in Heaven.

If we did not have the Holy Spirit, we could not have the ability to feel and communicate God's love. We would not be able to so easily understand the difference from right and wrong, or good and evil.

Have the crew leaders empty their bags. There are random assortments of items in the bags. Everything from string, to bandaids to coffee filters or empty containers and pots.

They may seem confused by the variation of items.

Read to the children: You all seem confused. Let me explain. You see, surviving in the woods has a kind of Trinity as well. That means there are three crucial things that we need for survival. Does anyone know what those are? (Allow kids to offer answers). The Trinity of survival is food, water, and shelter. Without these things, we cannot survive. Just like our spirit cannot survive without the Holy Trinity.

Today, we are going to start our survival journey by building a survival shelter. Do you see any items here that will help us build a shelter?

Assist the kids in choosing adequate items. Twine, blanket, and cloth coverings

Survival Shelter

*Weather permitting, this may take place outdoors.

Supplies needed:

Several sticks around 5 foot long OR pool noodles would work.

Various items from crew leaders' bags.

Shelter:

I recommend using the lean-to triangle shelter style, for timely purposes. A picture of ours is provided. You can also be creative and try other ways as you wish.

To build:

1. First you will need to secure the center. Using a large forked limb, drive the "post" into the ground just enough to stabilize it (we used large logs to help secure it as well). Make sure to leave the "forked" side up, or if you have a forked tree you can use this as your base instead.

2. Using a long and sturdy limb, lean it in between the forked base. Now you should have the beginning of a lean to.

3. Using approximately five foot long sticks, lean them against the long stick. (You're working on a triangular shaped skeleton). As you add to it, it will take more shape and become more sturdy.

Each group can add to the survival shelter as they see fit. Consider ways to keep out pests, small animals, or build some kind of slightly elevated bed to place a sleeping bag on. Blocking wind and weather is a big factor. Different groups may add different features.

Moss, leaves and mud are typically used to seal this kind of shelter, however students can pretend with other items such as paper and strips of cloth.

*NOTE! Do *not* be intimidated by building a shelter! It does *not* need to be perfect! The most important thing is that the kids are having fun and using team work. I recommend the triangular-shaped shelter for a couple reasons, but it also adds emphasis to the idea that "trinities" have strength. If the example shelter is more than what you want to do, here is another suggestion:

Alternative Blanket shelter:

Use a long string or rope and tie it between two trees or sturdy places (if indoors). Drape a blanket or table cloth over the rope and tug it into a triangular shaped shelter just big enough to sleep in. This will obviously take much less time, but you can have kids add things to it and plan out their campsite (barriers to keep critters out or brainstorming things they could sleep on, for example).

WOODLAND GAMES-DAY 1

Read to the children: Welcome to Woodland Games! I hear you all have lost yourselves in the woods, is that true? (Allow kids to answer). Wow! It sounds like you've had quite an eventful evening so far. But I have great news! Even when we are lost..(God leads the way!). That's right! God is our guide.

But guess what? Even when we get ourselves in these icky situations, we can still try to enjoy every moment. And so we are going to explore some ways to help *others* find us in the wild when we are lost, and hopefully we have fun while we practice!

If you were to get lost in the woods, the best thing you can do is sit down and think. So let's try that right now. (Allow kids to sit down). THINK very hard about what you would do if you were looking for someone in the woods. (Have kids shout out ideas for what they would look for). Those are all very good suggestions!

If I were looking for one of you, the first thing I would do is look at the last place I saw you. So if you're sitting down, it may be easier for your friends or your parents to find you! If you're always moving, that makes it difficult for your searchers. But there are times when you may need to move.

Maybe there is bad weather coming, or a long time has passed and it's getting dark, or you think you need to move to a safer place. So if you're going to move, what is something you can do to help others track you? (Allow kids to offer answers). If you move, you should *always* mark your trail. That's what we are going to practice doing today!

Hide and Seek with a Twist

Supplies needed:

Crepe paper, rocks, sticks, pieces of fabric, and other misc. items that can be used to mark a trail.

How to play:

1. Break into groups of two or three

2. Determine who will be the hiders and searchers. (Label the searchers as a rescue team for added importance).
3. The first group of hiders will use varieties of "trail marker items" to mark their trail and hide.
4. Meanwhile, the chosen "rescue team" should either be blindfolded or with their backs turned. They can count to sixty or so (time at leaders discretion).
5. The "rescue team" (another group of two or three—do NOT send the entire class to search at the same time) will look for clues and try to find the hiders.

 The goal is for the second group to find them in less than 15 or 20 seconds (time can be at station leaders' discretion).

Groups will take turns repeating this activity. Once they get the hang of the game, they can make it more challenging for the seekers by using smaller and more discreet clues. The goal is to make kids more observant and pay attention to their surroundings while also challenging them to think about ways to help others find them if they are lost.

Shelter Animals

Supplies needed:

Hula Hoops or pool noodles to make "cages"

How to play:

1. One person will be assigned as the "Forest Ranger".

2. Another person will be assigned as a "Bad wolf".

3. The remaining students will divide themselves up as different animals; such as, rabbits, squirrels, and birds. The stations are "cages" that the forest ranger has set up for the different animal groups to keep them safe from a big predator on the loose, the wolf!

4. The "animals" all start in the assigned cages.

5. When the station leader says, "Go!" The wolf will begin to release the animals from the cages by tagging them.

6. The "animals" all then run all around like crazy!

7. The Forest Ranger's job is to tag the animals and put them back into their cages! But the wolf can continue to release the animals by simply tagging them in their cages. Watch chaos ensue and listen to the laughter! Change out forest rangers and wolves occasionally.

***Note**: it is important to express the importance of playing nicely and fair with others. Pushing with two hands and other aggressiveness should not be allowed during this game. To "tag" someone means to simply touch them with your hand—not push.

DAY 1 CAMP CLOSING (script)

Leader: Good evening everyone! Wow, it has been such an eventful day and everyone looks like they have been busy! It is hard work when you've gotten yourself (and all your friends) lost in the woods. But that's ok, because even when we are lost…(God leads the way!)

That's right. And I think we learned quite a bit today about some ways that God leads us when we are lost! We learned how compasses work, how important the Holy Trinity is…can anyone tell me what the "Holy Trinity of survival" is? (Allow kids to answer)

That's right. It is food, water and shelter. (Yawn dramatically). And I sure hope you prepared a good shelter because I am *so* tired.

Rowdy Woods (from behind stage): Haha! Tired?

Leader turns around dramatically: Did you just hear that? Someone—

Rowdy: Ha ha ha! It was me! (Exits from a cave/makeshift shelter on stage) My name is Rowdy Woods! Who are all these kids and people?

Leader: Oh hello! We are enjoying a week of VBS, but we got lost. Who are you? Are you here to help us find our way out of the woods?

Rowdy: Ha ha! Help you? I think not. I am sorry to tell you, but there is no hope for you now. I've been here for fifteen years and no one's ever bothered helping me! Why should I help the lot of you?

Leader: You were lost fifteen years ago? And you're still here? Wow, you must be great at survival! You could help us with that!

Rowdy: Bah! That's right. I am a man of the woods. I don't ever want to leave! In fact, I lost myself on purpose!

Leader: You lost yourself… on purpose? But why?

Rowdy: (awkwardly) I had some troubles. I…I…couldn't take it any more.

Leader: Rowdy, could you tell us more?

Rowdy: It was robots!

Leader: Robots caused you to get lost in the woods??

Rowdy: No…well yes. But not exactly. (Sits down on a log) You see, I had it all. I was *rich*! I had a good job, a big house, nice cars, and I went on big vacations every other month!

Leader: Well, what happened?

Rowdy: The robots took over! They took my job away and I…I got angry and I ran away. I left every thing behind and decided I don't care if I ever go back to the city again! The robots can have the city and everything in it but they can't have me!

Leader: Wow, Rowdy, I am so sorry about this. It must be so hard for you! But…I have to say, this sounds so familiar. (Looks out into the audience) Does Rowdy's story sound familiar to anyone else here?

(Relate his story to the book of Job)

Today, we just learned about someone who had something similar happen to them. It was about a man named Job who lost his farmhands to an invasion and his business struggled.

Rowdy: Was it a robot invasion?

Leader: Um, no not quite.

Rowdy: (shakes his head sadly). Wow, that must have been sad.

Leader: It was. But the good news is, that God was always there for him! And we know that even when we are lost…(God leads the way!)

Rowdy: (falls off his log, blown away by the loudness) God whatta whatty? Leads the way?

Leader: That's right. God is like a way maker. And even though we are a little worried sometimes, we know that we can lean on Him and he will eventually lead us back to where we're meant to be. You know what? I think we should sing Rowdy Woods a song about God!

Lead the kids in music.

When the song has been practiced through several times, release the students to go home.

BIBLE ADVENTURES DAY 2

Supplies needed: light craft supplies from OT or glow sticks and string and beads for glowing necklaces.

Daily affirmation: Even when we are anxious….*God leads the way!*

*Note: It may be helpful to have a drawing (even if it's not great!) of this scene on a white board. Kids will appreciate any form of art to help them understand a story! For added engagement, you can draw blank faces on stick figures and call up volunteers to draw either happy or sad faces that are appropriate to the emotions being discussed in the story.

Read to the children: Good evening everyone! I am so glad that you have returned to this very special place that we have found in the woods! I heard that you all built a survival shelter yesterday. Is that true? (Allow children to answer)

That is wonderful. But it must be so strange, maybe even scary, to sleep somewhere so far from home. Have any of you ever stayed somewhere that wasn't at home? (Allow children to answer) Yes, sometimes when we are far from home for very long we can become *anxious*. To be anxious means to feel worried. But that is okay, it is normal to feel anxious sometimes. And we know that even when we are anxious….*God leads the way!*

That's right! Today in Bible Adventures we are going to learn more about Job. Poor Job. He had it all! And then Satan began to torment him, hoping to cause Job to lose his faith in God. But did Job lose his faith in God yesterday? (Allow children to answer) No! He did not. But that was not the end of Job's story.

Yesterday, a messenger came to Job's home to tell him that all of his farm hands had died and his animals had gone. Before this messenger was even done speaking, yet *another* messenger came rushing into the home to Job. He cried frantically, "The fire of God fell from the skies fell and burned up the sheep and the servants, and consumed them! I alone have escaped to tell you!"

While the second messenger was still speaking, a *third* messenger came rushing in: "The Chaldeans formed three bands, raided the camels and took them away! And then killed the servants with the edge of the sword. I am the only one left!

To say that Job was feeling rather anxious is an understatement. But unfortunately, Satan still was not done. Soon, another messenger came to see Job and he was obviously in great distress. He said to Job, "Your sons and daughters were having a feast in their oldest brother's house, and suddenly a great wind came across the wilderness. It struck the corners of the house and it fell onto the young people. They have all died."

Say to the children: It sounds like Satan is really trying hard to weaken Job. Do you think that he will succeed? (Allow kids to answer).

Do you think that Job was feeling anxious? Yes I think Job was very anxious. Even when we are anxious….*God leads the way*! Let's take a moment to think about what we would do if we were in this situation. It would be very easy to become sad, and angry and even question God.

Job's light of life seemed to go out. He was so very sad. But even still, he did not curse God. He could still see that God was like a bright light in the darkness of his life.

Light craft

Follow instructions on OT light craft of choice.

SURVIVING THE WOODS DAY 2

Daily affirmation: Even when we are anxious….*God leads the way!*

Supplies needed:

Rocks

Sticks and/or logs

Fire kindle

Optional: s'mores stuff for added fun!

Say to the children: Welcome back to Surviving the Woods! (Stretch out back, dramatically) Wow, that was quite the night sleeping in that fantastic shelter you built last night. It's a good thing we have a skilled group of kids here.

Yesterday when you were here, we learned about the Holy Trinity and how it's similar to surviving in the wild! Can anyone tell me what the Holy Trinity is? (Allow kids to answer) Yes, it is the Father, the Son, and the Holy Spirit. And we cannot live without those things! Whether we realize they are there or not, they are the very reason we wake up every day.

But there is another Trinity we learned about yesterday. It is called the Trinity of Survival. Can anyone remind me of what those things were? (Allow kids to answer). That's right, it is food, water, shelter.

Today we are going to learn about *another* Trinity. I know, that's a lot isn't it? Today, we are going to learn how to build a fire! Let's think of some ways that having a fire might be helpful to survive in the woods. (Allow children to offer suggestions…for warmth, to cook food, to keep bugs and critters away, alert someone to your whereabouts, etc.) Yes, having a fire is very helpful. And it is the first thing you should be thinking of after food, shelter, and water.

Before we learn about the three things it takes to build a good fire, let's prepare our fire area.

Take the provided rocks and create a fire ring (have kids help you) While you're doing this explain the importance of clearing away brush before starting a fire. Also, briefly discuss when it would *not* be a good time to start a fire (very windy and/or dry conditions). If it is windy, the tiniest spark of a fire can set an entire forest on fire and in that case, you would have much bigger problems on your hands! In this area of the states, burn bans are not as common as they are out West.

Say to the kids: Now that we have our fire area prepared, let's talk about some ways we can start a fire. There are three things that a fire needs to survive: oxygen, fuel, and heat. So let's start by gathering some fuel and setting it right here by the fire area. (Send kids to pick up sticks, nearby logs and brush. If the station is inside, have these things scattered about the room so the kids feel like they are gathering things up). The station leader should be the primary person to assemble the "fire", but can call on one or two students to help at a time.

Build the fire in your preferred fashion.

At this time, ask the crew leaders to empty their bags again. Ask them for a toilet paper roll, dryer lent, and Vaseline. Demonstrate how to many a quick and efficient fire starter by stuffing the lent into the toilet paper roll, and adding a small amount of Vaseline to the ends.

Using the Station Leader's preferred method of lighting, "light" the fire.

*Please note: whether real fire or pretend fire is used is dependent on the station leader's comfort and skill level/local church rules. Children will be perfectly happy with building a pretend fire, so if you do not have someone at your church who is comfortable building a real fire or it isn't feasible to do so, don't sweat it. In fact, it is recommended to use a pretend fire for the preschool and kindergarten age groups.

Once the fire is "taking off", explain that in order for this fire to survive it has to have all three things, and encourage them to brainstorm things they could do if the fire starts to die. (Add more dry brush, fan it to give it air, stack logs in a way that retains heat.

WOODLAND GAMES DAY 2

Daily affirmation: Even when we are anxious…*God leads the way!*

Supplies needed:

Several ropes or jump ropes

A set (or a few sets) of Googly eyed goggles.

Bandana, if desired

Miscellaneous items for obstacles such as Hula hoops, pool noodles, etc.

Say to the children: Welcome back to Woodland games! Wow, I heard that you built a shelter and slept in it last night! I'm very impressed!

But, my! You all must be so scared! So worried! So *anxious*. But I want to tell you something: even when we are anxious…*God leads the way*!

(Surprised) Oh. It seems like you already knew that!

Survival Ropes

Play a game of tug of war with a triple braided rope. Before the game begins, recite to the students "A triple braided cord is not easily broken." Then have the kids participate in a game of tug of war.

Googly-eyed obstacles.

This game can also use a blindfold instead if Googly eyes are not available. Use the miscellaneous items such as pool noodles, hula hoops, etc. to set up an obstacle course. Start simple (especially with younger students) and increase the challenge with every round. The kids will get a good giggle out of watching each other try to complete the obstacle with Googly eyes on. Be sure to demonstrate to the kids before you begin, so they know exactly what they should be doing.

After a couple rounds have been completed, talk about how difficult it is to do tasks when our vision is impaired. It would be much easier to understand where we were going if we just had some help. And allow them to have a friend help guide them along and notice the difference.

Just like these friends were helpful here, God is helpful each and every day that we allow Him to lead the way.

CAMP CLOSING DAY 2

Leader: Welcome back to camp, friends! Wow you all look so exhausted! You must have had a busy day! It's so good to see you all back here. I have spent all day wondering…pacing… thinking… I have been so worried about you! But that's okay, because even when you are anxious….*God leads the way!*

Right, exactly. You must be learning so much about surviving the woods. Did anyone figure out how to build a fire? Because I really don't want to sleep in the dark again tonight. Or get bit by bugs…and it would be nice to have something to cook a fish or two on.

You know, today I realized something! There seems to be a trend to survival. It is…the number three. We need three things to survive…(have kids join you in listing) food, water, shelter. Right! And today we learned about fire. It also takes *three* things for fire to survive. Those things are…(kids join you in listing off) oxygen, fuel, and heat!

And there was another thing that caught my attention. It was something about a triple braided cord. "A triple braided cord is not easily broken". Yes, jump ropes braided together are very strong!

And last but not least…the Holy Trinity. Can anyone tell me what the Holy Trinity is? (Call on a student to answer) Yes, it is the Father (point up) the Son (point down) and the Holy Spirit (make a circle around yourself and ask the students to do the same). We could not exist without these three things!

Rowdy Woods enters, nervously humming to himself while preparing a (pretend) fire. He appears to be ignoring the group entirely.

Leader: Rowdy? Hi Rowdy!

Rowdy pauses squeezes his eyes shut, apparently willing the group to disappear. He repeats this action several times, hoping to open his eyes to nothing.

Leader: Rowdy, it's us! The group of explorers you met yesterday.

Rowdy sighs exasperatedly.

Rowdy: I thought you all would be gone by now! What are you doing still lingering around my camp?

Leader: We are *lost,* Rowdy! But I have to say, I'm beginning to see why you like it so much out here. The trees are beautiful..

Rowdy: Beautiful?

Leader: It's peaceful…

Rowdy: It *was* peaceful, you mean.

Leader: The food is good, the games are fun…

Rowdy: Games? Fun? What kind of survivalist are you? There's no time for fun and games!

Rowdy continues to work on his fire, appearing nervous and frequently checking over his shoulder.

Leader: Uh, Rowdy? Are you okay? You seem nervous.

Rowdy: It's nothing. I'm busy! Can you all just go away now?

Leader: Rowdy, your hands are shaking. Are you anxious about something?

Rowdy: Anxious? Doesn't that mean worried? No! I am not scared of the dark!

Leader: No one said you were scared of the dark…

Rowdy: We'll I'm not!

Still shaking and working nervously.

Leader: So you *are* afraid of the dark! Rowdy…that's okay because we know that even when we are anxious…*God leads the way!*

Rowdy drops his things, shocked by the noise.

Rowdy: Right. So…what does God have to do with being stuck out in the woods and listening to scary noises all night long in the dark?!

A coyote howls in the distance.

Leader: It has everything to do with it! God is the one who created this place. And all the animals and creatures in it! Not only that, but you don't have to be afraid of the dark. Because God is always with you. He is like a light in the darkness.

Rowdy: Bet that guy Job, who you told me about yesterday, didn't think so.

Leader: Actually, we learned more about Job today. *(Gesture to the kids)* What happened to Job today? (Allow them to answer) Yes, Job lost several more of his employees and even his own children to terrible tragedies.

Rowdy: Wow, that's so sad.

Leader: It is. But do you know what? Job still did not stop believing in and honoring God. He loved God very much. And even through all that darkness in his life, he kept his eyes on God, who was like his light. In fact, today we made something really neat that shows God's light.

Shut the lights off, and allow kids to show off their light craft that they made in Bible Adventures.

Rowdy pauses, and is briefly in awe of their lights.

Rowdy: Wow! I can see it! But…I…I don't know. I'm still pretty anxious…I mean—

Leader: Rowdy, it's normal to feel worried sometimes. But if we learned one thing today, it's that even when we are anxious…*God leads the way!*

Rowdy is blown away by the noise.

Rowdy: It's so hard to see in the dark. It's hard to know where you're going…(looks over shoulder) or what's watching…I have to admit that I'm glad you all have lights so I can see better.

Leader: It's always nice to have friends who are willing to help. But do you know what? There is no friend like our amazing God. Sometimes it's easy to forget that He is always there and willing to lead the way for us.

Rowdy: But how do I know where he's leading me at all? Or where he's leading me? Does he reach out and grab my hand? Will I hear his voice?

Leader: Those are great questions! To me, the easiest way to know that God is leading me is to always make my everyday choices good ones. I always ask myself…is it good? Is it kind? Is it true? And if it is…I think that's the way God wants me to go.

Rowdy: Wow. I never thought of it that way before. So I suppose you don't think me shouting at robots and all those people who invented them was such a good idea?

Leader: Maybe not the best. But it's okay because God still loves you anyway, and will forgive you. Sometimes making the right choice is hard to do. But we should always try. Just know that no matter what you do…know that even when we are anxious…*God leads the way!*

Lead group in music.

At our church, Rowdy Woods was musical and helped lead music. That's not a requirement–but it did make it really fun for the kids!

BIBLE ADVENTURES DAY 3

Supplies needed:

Daily affirmation: Even when things get messy…*God leads the way!*

Read to the children: Welcome back to Bible Adventures! Wow it has been such an adventurous week! And I am so glad that you all have come back to visit me. Did you all meet a new friend today out here in the woods? (Allow children to answer). Yes! You met Bobby the Beaver!

I know Bobby the Beaver, he is a good friend of mine. But I have to say, the first time that I met him I was not sure about him. He was a very messy critter. But I soon learned that I should not be so hard on Bobby. He is a wonderful piece of God's creation. But I'm getting ahead of myself…

You have come back here to learn more about our friend Job! Poor old Job. Last night we learned that not only did Job lose his workers and all his prosperity, but he lost his children! Now Job was terribly distraught over this tragedy. He was so sad. But can you believe it, after all that, still Job did not curse God. He still loved God very much!

Now, how frustrated do you think Satan was that his plan was not working? He wanted to turn Job away from God, and Job simply would not turn away. Talk about faith! But do you know what else? Satan still did not give up. He was determined to turn Job against God.

So now that Job had lost his servants, his success, and his children, Satan wanted to cause Job harm. God forbid Satan from taking Job's life, so instead Satan caused a sickness to fall over Job. This caused him to break out into several very painful sores. He was in terrible pain.

And do you know what his wife said to him? "Why don't you just curse God and die?"

That wasn't very nice was it? It seemed as if Satan was even using Job's own wife as his mouthpiece. That means Satan was causing her to say exactly what he wanted to say to Job. (Remember Satan is invisible to Job). And Satan knew that Job's wife had a lot of influence over him.

What do you think Job did? (Allow kids to offer answers)

Job *still* did not curse God. Instead, he said to his wife, "Haven't you any faith? God is great!"

Now this did not mean that Job was not miserable, because he was. Not only was he mourning the loss of so many that he loved, but he was also dealing with his own illness. He pondered why such things would happen to him. And he was not the only one.

Several of Job's friends came to visit him during this intense season of mourning (that means a time of sadness and remembering the things he lost). And when they came, I am sure they were shocked to see the *mess* that Job was living in. And let's just say they had some questions.

(Using your fingers, count off the misfortunes with the kids' help). So Job had a huge farm operation with several animals and servants. His servants were killed, the animals were run off, *more* workers were killed, his children all died, and now he's dealing with an illness. That's a lot of bad stuff. Can you imagine what his farm operation would look like if suddenly all the workers had died and many animals escaped?

It very quickly became a *mess*. The weeds were probably over grown, the food was scarce, and the money income was not much. Do you think Job's friends were surprised? (Allow children to answer).

Yes I am sure they were very surprised! And it may have been easy to arrive and make some judgements about Job's situation. But if we learn one thing from our friend Bobby the Beaver today, it is that we should not judge others for the way they live their lives. Bobby the Beaver makes a mess when he is redirecting waterways, but he is serving God the way he was meant to. And sometimes other people do things that seem strange to us. But we may not understand their situation.

(If desired, go over a few examples—see a messy yard with tall grass? Maybe they are sick and need help mowing. See a person in a wheel chair? Perhaps they were in an accident. Etc.)

Tomorrow, we will learn some more about Job's friends and what they had to say. Also we will learn how Job grieved *and* how the ending of his story turned out! But now it is time to do a fun activity.

Water Way Experiment

Materials needed:

Aluminum baking pans
Aluminum foil
Rocks
Sticks

How to build your waterway:
First, have a helper help pass out the materials. Have one example already prepared so that you can show the students what to expect. **Place students in pairs**.

Each group should receive:
1. Aluminum pan
2. Aluminum foil
3. Rocks
4. Sticks

Let the students know that their waterway is their own, and they get to make it however they want. They will bend the aluminum foil to manipulate it into rivers or streams. They can use sticks and rocks to add to their landscape. They can even use pea gravel in their waterways if they wish.   NO WATER WILL BE USED UNTIL THEY ARE DONE.

When everyone is finished, you or an adult helper, will go around with a water pitcher and try out each water way.

As they are working and during your demonstration, explain how rivers are good for the environment. They provide an important habitat for fish, fresh water supply, irrigation, transportation, etc.

SURVIVING THE WOODS DAY 3

Daily affirmation: Even with things get messy…*God leads the way!*

Note: This lesson requires careful supervision. It is important to not allow students to drink their dirty water.

Materials needed:

Pitcher of water
Pan
Food coloring or pitcher of muddy water
Sand
Small rock pebbles or gravel (crew leader bags)
Activated charcoal (crew leader bags)
Coffee filters (crew leader bags)
Cotton balls
Strips of t shirt fabric
Plastic soda or water bottle
Scissors
Water "contaminants" (glitter, oil, beads, dirt etc.)

Say to the children: Welcome back to Surviving the Woods! You all are becoming such pros at surviving out here. We are on day three. And that means you're doing pretty good so far! But there is something about day three that is very important to know when it comes to surviving the woods.

By day three of being lost in the wilderness , you *need* to have found water. Did you know that the human body can only survive three days without water? Yes, water is very important to have in order to survive! And God provided us with plenty of it. Around 70 percent of our world is water. That water provides us with ways to drink, to travel, and many organisms grow in water that actually provide most of the world with its oxygen supply.

It is important for us to take care of God's wonderful water systems.

Unfortunately, over the years, humans have made some pretty big messes and a lot of our water systems are in danger. But what did we learn today? That even when things get messy…*God leads the way!* That's right. Our water systems have been contaminated with chemicals and harmful things that not only hurt our fish and wildlife, but they also are harmful to us if we drink it!

Regardless of how clean a body of water or stream is, we still need to clean it. This is not only because of possible chemical contaminants, but also because there are natural bacterias in unclean water that can make us very sick if we drink it. And when we're stuck out on the woods the last thing we need is for us to get really sick and dehydrated.

Instruct students to create their own dirty water: Give them each large cups and fill them with water. They can mix and add several items to it, creating "dirty" water. Messes will likely be made. Remember to be patient when this happens, and use the opportunity to reiterate today's affirmation: Even when things get messy…*God leads the way!*

Have crew leaders empty their bags again. Take out the coffee filters, charcoal, sand and rocks.

Say to the children: Today we are going to explore ways to filter some water! There are many ways to filter water. But today we're going to learn some ways we can do it with minimal materials. One way you can quickly and easily filter water is by using what we call a Life Straw. Show them a Life Straw. If you are ever out camping or hiking, it's a good idea to carry one of these in your pack. All you have to do is put the end of it in some water and use it just like a straw. The straw has filters in it that will clean almost any kind of water and make it safe to drink.
*Note: make sure to inform the kids that these will not work on salt water. Salt water is what makes up the oceans and it is far too salty for us to consume. It would cause dehydration. Never try to drink salt water.
Show the kids a pan. Another way you can help make water safe to drink is by boiling it. Your parents may boil water often when they are cooking. You can use a pan like this and hold it over a fire, or you can also use a metal cup. Hold it (or hang it) over the fire so that the water is bubbling and hot for about ten minutes. You will need something that is fireproof and that tolerates heat! Should we use plastic? (Allow kids to answer). No. It will melt! Should we use wood? (Allow kids to answer). Probably not. It can burn!

Hold up the pitcher of dirty water. How many of you would like to drink this dirty water? (Allow kids to answer). Yes, it's pretty icky looking. Hold up a pitcher of clean water. How many of you would drink this water? (Allow kids to answer) Yes it is much cleaner. But now, I need to turn this water (the dirty water) into this water (the clean water)! Let's see what happens when we build our own filter!

See next page for full instructions.

Build Your Own Water Filter

Step 1: Cut off bottom of plastic bottle and place upside down in a tall vase or drinking glass

Step 2: Stuff cotton balls, cloth, or a coffee filter as the first layer. The first layer should be about one to two inches thick.

Step 3: Add an inch of activated charcoal as second layer on top of cotton layer.

Step 4: Over the charcoal, add about two inches of the gravel or rocks as the third layer.

Step 5: Add about three to four inches of clean sand on top of the gravel.

Step 6: Add gravel to bottle on top of sand as the final layer.

Step 7: Add their homemade dirty water.

Because sometimes the filtration takes a while (it drips) the kids will need to leave their water filters behind. They can pour their water in and when they return the next day everyone can evaluate how well their water filters cleaned the water.

Explain to the children that even after filtering water in this way, it is very important to boil it to kill any dangerous bacteria.

WOODLAND GAMES DAY 3

Daily affirmation: Even when things get messy…*God leads the way!*

Say to the children: Welcome back to Woodland Games! Roll your sleeves up, survivalists, because we might get a little messy. But that's okay because even when things get messy… *God Leads the Way!*

Materials needed:

• *2-4 pools*

• *Sponges*

• *Pool noodles*

• *Pitchers or cheap, single spout watering cans*

Water Sponge Relays

Preparation

1. Place four pools on either side of the relay course.

2. Fill two pools on one side with water and water balls.

3. Place the empty pools on the opposite side (starting line).

4. Put the kids into two teams. At the whistle, the kids will run to the other side and collect water using the sponges or balls. They will race back to the empty pool and empty the water into their pools. Allow them to repeat as many rounds as you see fit. At the end of the game, compare the amount of water in the starting pools to determine the winning team.

Note: cups or sand buckets can be used instead of balls, if desired.

 *Shake it up! Have students try different ways to collect and distribute water. Using a minimum of two pool noodles and a watering can, they can collect and pour water into the pool that way. This will require team work!

Log Limbo

Use pool noodles and have helpers hold the "logs" to do a log limbo. After each round (when everyone has gone through) lower the log. See how low the kids can go without touching the log!

CAMP CLOSING DAY 3

Leader: Welcome back to camp friends! Wow! It has been three days and you all are starting to look a little messy! Today we learned about beavers, God's amazing water system, how to clean dirty water, *and* we learned a bit more about our friend Job, who had a terrible mess to live in!

Poor old Job! He was living in such sadness. And his farm operation was falling apart! The grass was overgrown, the fields were neglected..and Job was covered in sores! What a mess! But even when things get messy…*God leads the way!*

That's right. Job knew that God was still—

(Interrupted by some kind of commotion going on off stage)

Leader: it sounds as if our friend…

Rowdy Woods is yelling and fighting with someone or something.

Leader: Rowdy? Is that you?

Rowdy appears, struggling with what appears to be a skunk.

Rowdy: it's a skunk! (Runs back and forth across stage, avoiding the skunk. Eventually, the skunk disappears behind the stage again. Rowdy claps his hands together smugly).

Rowdy: And *that* is how you handle an intruder. (Claps his hands together smugly)

Leader: Hello, Rowdy. It's good to see you again.

Rowdy: And I wish I could say the same to you lot. Are you *ever* going to go back home?

Leader: Rowdy, we are lost. We can't find our way home.

Rowdy: That's right! You'll never get out of this mess. This woods is never ending. You make yourself at home here or you'll sink.

Leader: Uh Rowdy? I hear something rustling around in the weeds over there. I think it's that skunk.

Rowdy: (struts over to the weeds and bends over to look at the apparent skunk).

 Hey there little buddy, I thought I told you it was time to go home— (on cue, the skunk "sprays" Rowdy with colored powder). Ahhh!!! It just sprayed me!

Jena Robertson
Copyright 2023

Leader: Uh oh, Rowdy. Looks like you've got a big mess to clean up. But that's okay because even when things get messy…*God Leads the Way!*

Rowdy: Okay, okay! God leads the way! I get it. But what am supposed to do with this mess?

Leader: Well, the first thing you could do is pray.

Rowdy: And how am I supposed to do that?

Leader: Think of God as your very best friend. Even though you may not always see him, he is always there listening.

(Meanwhile, Rowdy is rummaging around his camp, looking for a way to clean himself up.)

 Rowdy: If he's listening, why doesn't he always answer?

Leader: God always answers in some way. As Job said, God is always faithful. But we can sometimes be impatient.

Rowdy: Right. (Wiping himself off)

Leader: I think Rowdy could use a little morale booster. Let's sing him a song!

BIBLE ADVENTURES DAY 4

Daily Affirmation: Even when we are confused…*God leads the way!*

Read to the children: Welcome back to Bible Adventures! I am so happy to see that you all have survived the woods so well! Today I heard that you all met another new friend—Skippy the Squirrel! Can anyone tell me what you learned about Skippy the Squirrel? (Allow children to answer).

Yes, Skippy is an amazing part of God's creation. But God made him special too. He is well known for being forgetful and becoming confused about where he hides his treasures, which are things like acorns and nuts. But because of that, new forests are able to grow! Even when we are confused…*God leads the way!*

*D*o you know someone else who was confused? (Allow kids to offer answers). I will tell you. It was Job! Yesterday we learned more of Job's sad story. He became ill and his own wife told him to just curse God and die! That's some pretty bad advice for a man who is suffering.

But Job's wife was not the only one who gave him bad advice. Several of his friends heard of his tragedies and came to visit him from far away. They were shocked to see the state of Job's business and Job himself, who was grieving terribly. Of course at this time, Job was vocalizing his confusion. He said things like, "Why me? What have I done to deserve this terrible fate?" And he also was angry with himself, and didn't want to live any longer. But God would not allow Satan to take Job's life. Job's life on earth was very special to God.

In the mean time, Job's friends offered their thoughts. Unsure how to comfort Job, they began offering up their theories to him as to why these bad things happened. The first friend said, "Go and confess your sins to the Lord…perhaps you have done something to deserve this…"

The second friend, whose name was Bildad, said, "Your children must have sinned, that's why they died!"

But Job knew that this was not true.

Another friend named Zophar said, "But nothing is stronger than God! Keep your eyes on God, Job!"

And this went on for quite some time. Let's just say that Job's friends offered lots of advice and also strange theories that were confusing. They wanted so badly to comfort him! They left Job feeling even more frustrated and *confused*. But in the end…Job never cursed God. He never turned against God and he never doubted God's good will. Job had *faith*. Faith is when you believe in something with all your heart and you stand strongly by that belief, never allowing anyone or anything to change your mind.

During this long period of grieving all of his losses and living in utter confusion, Job spent a lot of time praying and talking to God. He could have done many other things, but instead he invested even *more* time praying! So…how do you think that made Satan feel?

Did Satan win? (No). Let's just say that Satan's plan did not work. No matter how hard he tried, he could not make Job turn away from God. Satan was furious! He lost at his own wicked game. God was pleased with Job. And at the end of Job's story, he was blessed with a new family, more children and new prosperity (success).

Discuss: So what did we learn about Job's story? (Allow children to answer). We learned that Satan never has good intentions. His goal is to turn everyone away from God. Satan represents evil and nothing that is good. God is the opposite of Satan. He, on the other hand, is always good and faithful. We make God happy when we have faith in him. We should be like Job and never give up on God, even if others around us tell us that we should. Occasionally, in life, we may be met with Satan's tricks. He may send something to us to try to turn us away from God. But when we feel like that is happening, we should get out our spiritual maps and find our way back to God.

Woodland Creatures Craft

Supplies needed:

Wooden slabs

Markers or paint

Station Leader: Pass out wooden slabs and help kids paint different animal prints on their wood pieces. On the back, write today's affirmation: "Even when we are confused…*God leads the way!*

SURVIVING THE WOODS DAY 4

Daily affirmation: Even when we are confused…*God leads the way!*

Say to the children: Welcome back to Surviving the Woods! It's been a long week. But each day that I see you, you look stronger..and wiser! But I have to say…you look hungry! Finding food out here in the wild is just not the same as opening the fridge.

Yesterday we learned how to make clean drinking water. Let's check out our hand made water filters and see how we did. (Allow children to observe yesterday's work and discuss for a moment or two).

Great! Now that we have shelter, water, and a warm fire…we're missing something. Can anyone tell me what we're missing? (Food).

That's right. We are missing food and I'm starting to get hungry! Finding safe food to eat in the wild is very important because it keeps our strength up. If we do not eat, we will lose the strength to do all the other necessary things to survive! Our body can go almost three weeks without food. However, it only takes hours before the lack of food causes us to grow weak… and *confused*. But even when we are *confused*….*God leads the way!*

So today we are going to explore some possible ways we can gather up some safe food to eat. What are some ways we could find food in the woods? (Allow children to offer answers).

Some ways we can find food in the woods are:

Hunting

Fishing

Finding safe and edible plants to eat

Nuts

Tell the children: It is very important to never put anything into your mouth that you are not absolutely sure of what it is. Many people have caused themselves to become sick by eating the wrong things. And let's just say getting sick while stranded in the woods is no fun! Learning about safe edible things from the woods takes years to perfect!

HUNTING AND FISHING ACTIVITY

*This is a great opportunity to enlist a guest dad, grandparent, or local outdoorsman to help out. The children will love seeing a new face and listening to their expertise.

Read the to the children: Today we're going to learn about some hunting and fishing skills. While there are many edible plants in the woods, they can be dangerous if you're not careful. If you hunt or fish, you are guaranteed food year round, and it will be the most fulfilling.

Fishing: Bring a fishing pole (or two) and allow kids to practice casting a fishing pole. A body of water is not needed—just use the practice weights that come with a children's fishing pole. Some may already know, but explain to all of them that when the bobber is pulled under that means that a fish has bitten the hook and it's time to reel it in!

**Preschoolers and kindergarteners may enjoy a magnetic fishing game better, as their motor skills are not quite as developed as older students. This is perfectly fine.

Hunting: Allow kids to practice their bow shooting skills with some amateur bows and targets. Toy bows and targets from the local toy store will also work perfectly fine. You can also make your own target. If there are higher quality bows and targets available, that is fine as well. Use at your own discretion and it is imperative for the station leader to assert safety and responsibility.

It is not recommended to use bladed arrows or real fishing hooks that would be used during an actual hunt. Remember that this is a church event and is only meant to *acquaint* the children with the idea, rather than perfect the skill. The ultimate goal of today's lesson is to show the kids God's abundance and see a glimpse at how well he provides for us in nature.

We happened to have a dad from the parish who had an abundance of practice bows and targets. He volunteered to bring his things and instructed the kids on how to shoot bows and arrows. This is not a requirement at all. Your shopping list will tell you to buy toy bows and fishing poles to play around with. **However, it's worth asking around at church to see if an outdoor enthusiast would volunteer to help on this day!

WOODLAND GAMES DAY 4

Daily affirmation: Even when we are confused…*God leads the way!*

Blinded Treasure Hunt Relays

Supplies needed:

2-4 small pools

Sand

Miscellaneous items

Acorns or "treasure" of choice

Object: The object of the game is for everyone to retrieve as many acorns as possible. They can keep the acorns (and plant them at home!)

Step 1:   Fill the pools with sand and bury the miscellaneous items and "treasures".

Step 2:   Divide the children into two groups and line them up directly across from a pool.

Step 3:   The first child(ren) will be blindfolded and then spun a couple times.

Step 4:   While still blindfolded, send the children to retrieve an acorn from the sand pile. When the first child returns, blindfold the next student to complete the task over and over until all have had a turn.

Step 5:   If children are struggling significantly with finding their way, have a team mate guide them along. And make note that it's much easier to find our way when we let God help lead us in this way.

Run Rabbit Run

Step1: Divide the group into two groups.

Step 2: Assign the first group to be the "rabbits" and line them all up beside each other on one side of the play yard.

Step 3: The second group will be the "foxes" and they will line up on the opposite side.

Step 4: the "Rabbits" will now follow a leading rabbit across the play yard. They must move in a single file line, and follow whatever steps the first rabbit takes. The rabbits also must make their way towards the foxes and cannot go backwards.

Step 5: The foxes will wait patiently, until they are ready to shout "Run rabbit Run!" Once that phrase is shouted, the foxes will chase the rabbits all the way back to the start line. Whoever is tagged becomes a fox.

CAMP CLOSING DAY 4

(Before you begin the closing program, have a bag of pretend fish that you "caught" today. Select a child from the crowd and when prompted, they will present it to Rowdy during the skit.) Optional: have blackberries, walnuts, and a paw paw to show during the second half of the skit.

Leader: Welcome back to our survival camp, Day 4! Can you believe we made it this long? The days and nights have been long. We have been tired. But with God's plentiful supplies, we were able to build a shelter. We have been cold, but God allowed us to build a fire for warmth. We have been thirsty, but God sent water! Today we were hungry, and God still provided for us! He is such an awesome God.

Today, we learned a little bit about Job and the end of his story. He was confused about why he had suffered all the terrible things when he was so faithful. He had no idea that Satan was taunting him. And his friends tried to be helpful by offering their opinions, but they only confused him more. The important thing is that Job was still faithful to God. We can all learn something from Job. That is that no matter what kind of pressure we are under from our peers, we should still trust in God.

Even when we are confused…*God Leads the Way!*

(Rowdy Woods enters, grumbling to himself)

Rowdy: (Exasperatedly) You've got to be kidding me. You're still here? *When* will you ever get a move on?

Leader: It's nice to see you too, Rowdy. How are you today?

Rowdy: Hungry.

Leader: Are you…hangry?

Rowdy: What does that even mean? All this modern folk talk.

Leader: Never mind. We're sorry that you're hungry. (Gesturing to Rowdy's hunting tools) It looks like you've just been hunting.

Rowdy: Thank you, Captain Obvious!

Leader frowns at Rowdy.

Rowdy: Sorry, I just..I'm just so *confused*. I did everything right. I set the traps, sharpened the tools, camouflaged myself and all. And still didn't see anything! I think that there was too much *competition* in the woods today. (He shoots an accusing glare at the crowd).

Leader: Uh, sorry about that. It's okay Rowdy, some days you will have a harder time than others. Even when we are confused….*God Leads the way!*

Rowdy: (stumbles backwards) Ok! Ok! I get it, God leads the way. (Looks up to sky as if talking to God) God, will you lead the way and send me something to eat? Because I'm *hungry!*

Leader: Actually, I think our friends might have something for you.

(The kids who have a net of fish, berries, paw paws, walnuts, etc. will bring it forward and present it to Rowdy)

Rowdy: Wow! You found all these? Thank you! Thank you so–(changes his voice) I mean….*thanks*. You all aren't too bad are you? I mean…you're *okay*. I can roast these fish over the fire. Well, I'll see you. (Begins to exit the stage)

If you don't have these things available to you, or if you're uncomfortable with it, you can omit this part of the skit entirely and skip to the star line.*

Leader: But wait! We don't know what some of these things are. We were hoping that maybe you could help us!

Rowdy: (smugly) Oh! You need my expertise, you mean?

Leader: Well, kind of….could you?

Rowdy takes out a walnut.

Rowdy: this is called a black walnut. It comes off the tree. All you have to do is crack the shell and eat the "meat" inside.

Crowd: ooooooooohhhhhh!

Rowdy takes out a Paw Paw.

Rowdy: And this is a Paw Paw. Also called an Indiana Banana. They are deeeeelicious. They are usually ripe around late July through August. You can tell they are ripe when they can be easily shaken off a tree.

Crowd: Ohhhhhhhhh!

Rowdy: And last but not least, these are blackberries! A woodland favorite! They usually like to grow near sticker bushes and in wooded areas where there is also plenty of sunlight.

Crowd: Ohhhhhhhhh!

Rowdy offers a smug and surly smile at everyone.

Rowdy: Well enough of that, I'm out of here

***Leader**: But Rowdy! It's time for campfire worship! Don't you want to join us for some songs?

Rowdy reappears, exasperated.

Rowdy: Oh, fine!

Lead the children in their nightly music routine.

BIBLE ADVENTURES DAY 5

Daily affirmation: Even when we are surprised…*God leads the way!*

Read to the children: Welcome back to Bible Adventures! We have survived five whole days out in the woods! You all are becoming such experts. And I am so glad that you have come back to see me again–one last time before we find our way home.

Yesterday in Bible Adventures, we learned the end of Job's story. And we learned how it's so very important to trust God, no matter how many bad things might happen to us. Today I want to tell you another story. First, let me explain that Job lived during the time of the Old Testament, which means it was before the time of Jesus. Jesus had not yet come to earth to save us from our sins.

So many years after Job's life, Jesus Christ was born. He was raised by Mary and Joseph, and enjoyed being a carpenter alongside Joseph. That means that he worked with wood, and built things with his hands. You see, he lived a fairly quiet and humble childhood. But as he got older, it became more and more clear that Jesus was no ordinary man.

Around the time he began preaching God's word, Jesus went fishing with some friends, also known as his disciples. They went out on a boat in the middle of the sea. They had been out there for quite some time and Jesus decided to take a nap.

During his nap, a fierce storm rolled in. The waters became rocky and dangerous, splashing roughly against the boat, causing it to rock horribly. Thunder rolled and lightning began to flash. The strong winds caused the waters to become even more rough and waves began to soar high above the fishing boat. Jesus's disciples thought the sea would swallow them up at any moment!

How do you think Jesus' disciples felt? (Allow children to answer) Scared, is how they felt! And they were very surprised to have this storm sneak up on them so quickly! One disciple shook Jesus awake. "Jesus! The storm! Surely we will all die! Don't you care?

Jesus barely opened an eye.

The men were temporarily at loss for words.

Then Jesus only sighed and said casually, "Peace. Be calm."

And do you know what happened? The storm stopped! Suddenly the waters were calm and the winds and thunder faded away. The disciples were shocked! They said, "Who is this? Who even the wind and waters listen to?"

The answer is…he is *God!* Jesus is a part of God's Holy Trinity. He is "the son". When God sent himself to Earth, he sent himself in the form of a man.

So while Jesus appeared to be an ordinary man, he certainly was not. Though his voice sounded like an ordinary man, he was actually God speaking through a man's mouth. So of course the wind and the waters obeyed him!

God in Heaven is not a human man. But he sent himself to live within Jesus's body *as a man.* Does anyone know why he did this? (Allow children to offer answers) This is the only way that God could truly save the rest of mankind from their sins. When he died on the cross, he sacrificed himself so that we could all have a way into Heaven. And all we have to do is believe in Him. And trust in Him. Even in the hard times, we must trust in our Lord and Savior just like Job trusted God when Satan dared to torment him.

Even when we are surprised….*God leads the way!*

Right. So we should always remember that God is there for us, even when surprising things happen to us. And I'll bet that storm was surprising*!*

Cork Boat Craft

Supplies needed:

Wine bottle corks

Rubber bands

Popsicle sticks

Foam paper

Hot glue

Markers and/or crayons

OR

Cork boat kits (can be purchased online at Oriental Trading).

If you have purchased the kit, follow the instructions on the kit.

Otherwise here is how to make your own DIY Cork boat:

Step 1: Give each child three wine corks

Step 2: Place the corks side by side and use two rubber bands to wrap around them to secure them together.

Jena Robertson
Copyright 2023

Step 3: Slide a popsicle stick between the corks, securing it in place with some hot glue.

Step 4: The foam paper will be cut into "sails". Two slits or holes will need to be punctured on the sails in order to slide them into the popsicle sticks. The students may decorate their sails as they wish.

Step 5: If you have water bowls or small pools available, let the kids try them out and enjoy!

SURVIVING THE WOODS DAY 5

Daily affirmation: Even when we are surprised…*God leads the way!*

Preparation: Have a bag or large basket handy. Before hand, fill it with these items:

Bird figurine or toy

A turtle figurine or toy

Pine cone

A cow figurine or toy

A cat figurine or toy

A doll who is having a really bad hair day

A toy frog

A sailor toy or a sail boat toy

A flower

**Have a helper today, hang back out of sight or behind you somewhere. Give them a metal kitchen pan and have them hit the pan with a wooden spoon for every time you (the leader) say "thunder". Do not do this every time a child says thunder. It may get overwhelming! Go over the script with your helper so they know what to expect.

Read to the children: Welcome back to Surviving the Woods! I heard that there is a storm coming today! How many of you like storms? (Allow children to raise their hands) How many of you *don't* like storms? (Allow kids to raise their hands). Yes. Storms can be scary! With all the wind, the rain and the lightning and **thunder**…yes, they can be loud. And sometimes they can make us anxious. Other times, they can catch totally off guard. Storms can be surprising, but even when we are surprised, *God leads the way!*

Okay great. So we've been out here in the wild for an entire week. And we don't have any phones, any TV's, or even a newspaper to help us know what the weather is going to be like. Sure, it might be sunny one minute, but what about tonight or tomorrow? How can we predict the weather ourselves without all our fancy gadgets? I know that a storm is coming when I hear **thunder,** or when I see lightning flash. But sometimes **thunder** and lighting come really late! And we are not prepared!

So what are some ways that you all can think of that might help us predict the weather? (Allow children to raise hands and offer answers)

Those are all really great ideas. Do you see this bag right here? (Hold up the bag and shake it). I was told that it holds many answers. Let's each take a turn pulling out one item at a time, and then we will talk about how that item can help us predict the weather.

Please refer to the information below for the items retrieved:

*Feigning surprise and amazement at every item will help keep the kids interested and engaged.

Bird: Birds are a really good indicator of impending weather changes. When rain or storms are on the way, birds tend to fly low or hover in groups in fields or other lower areas—even on power lines. They can begin to do this up to three or four days in advance. Scientists believe that birds can sense the change in air pressure way up high in the sky, and that is why they choose to hang out in lower places. The pressure change hurts their ears! Birds will also get very quiet right before a storm begins.

Turtle: Have you ever been driving down the road with your parents and seen a turtle trying to cross the road? While turtles move around often (alas, slowly), they tend to look for "higher ground" right before it rains. Sometimes that means they end up on the roads, because most roads are built higher than other natural areas.

Pine cone: There is a saying that goes like this, "Open Pine, weather's fine." Pine cones can either close up or open up. If a pine cone is open, that means it's dry and probably going to be a dry day. If the pine cone begins to close, that means wet weather is coming.

Cow: It is said that many times right before big weather changes, several cows in a herd will lie down. So if you see a herd of cows all laying down in a pasture, be on the look out. It could also mean a baby calf is being born as well.

Cat: Can't find your cat? If your cat is hiding under the bed or in the closet or wherever cats like to hide…it may be because there is bad weather approaching. Cats have also been known to hide before an earthquake.

Doll with a bad hair day: Sometimes you might hear your mom say something like "my hair is so frizzy today!" That means it has lots of extra tiny curls. Our hair does this when there is a lot of moisture in the air. Summer time is often humid in this way. But some days it's worse than others! And on those days, keep your eyes and ears tuned because a storm could be lingering.

Frog: Frogs always croak louder right before a rain. Because frogs really like water, they get extra excited when they know rain is coming!

Sail boat: There is another old saying that goes like this, "Red sky in the morning, sailors take warning. Red sky at night, a sailor's delight." That is a saying because sailors, who are out on the sea, don't have anything to help them know the weather except the sky. And they have always known that a red sky in the morning means there are vapor clouds in the west and the sunlight is reflecting off of those, causing the sky to look really red. If it is red at night, that means the weather system has moved on past.

Flower: Flowers do two amazing things before rain. The first thing is that they smell much stronger. The second thing that some flowers do is begin to close their petals up. It is as if they are protecting themselves from the possible damage that the rain and wind might cause them.

Read to the children: Isn't it amazing, how God created all of nature? Each and every part of God's creation is designed to interact with one another. And because of this, we are all able to live on this amazing planet called Earth. So next time you're out walking in nature, look for some of these signs and see if you can predict the weather. Make a journal about the things you see, and see if you notice any patterns.

Quick pine cone experiment

If there is enough time, take the pine cone(s) and place it in some water. Watch as the pine cone expands. Explain that moisture does this to pine cones.

WOODLAND GAMES DAY 5

Daily affirmation: Even when we are surprised…*God leads the way!*

Messy Balloon Pop

Supplies needed:

Balloons

Confetti

Colored powder

Water

String or clothes line

Clamps or clothes pins

Toothpicks

How to play:

Step 1: Prepare and fill plenty of balloons ahead of time. Fill several balloons with confetti, some with colored powder, and others with water.

Step 2: Hang a cloths line or string up and attach filled balloons using the clothes pins or clamps (or tie them on with a string if need be.)

Step 3: Have students take turns choosing two balloons each. They cannot touch the balloons with their hands. They must rupture the balloons with a tooth pick. Did they guess right or were they *surprised*?

Note: You may want to have some safety glasses handy. Some kids may not enjoy powder or or confetti in their eyes.

CAMP CLOSING DAY 5

* Parents and families will be present for the program at this time.

Leader to all: Welcome to Lost in the Woods! It has been a wild week here at VBS, and let me just say that you all have some amazing kids! They are strong, courageous, and really great survivalists! I'd like to introduce you to the groups: First, we have the Bigfoot Squad (3-5th graders). Second, we have the Wolf Pack (1-2nd grade). And last, we have the Lil' Hooties (preschool-kindergarten)!

This week all started when we decided to take a little hike. We were marveling at God's beautiful creation when we suddenly found ourselves *lost!* Was it scary? Yes! Was it lonely? Well not quite. Was it boring? Not at all! Although we were so very afraid to be lost in the woods, we learned that even when we are lost…*God leads the way!*

That's right. And on our travels we also met some unexpected friends. We met some very wise woodland creatures, some awesome leaders, and even a hermit!

Lead children in song 1.

On day one, we knew that we needed to make a shelter fast. Our survivalist experts (feature to station leaders) advised us on what we called the Holy Trinity of Survival. You see, our relationship with God has three very important parts—The Father, the Son, and The Holy Spirit. Without those three things, our faith cannot thrive. And in order to survive in the wild, we also need three very important things to survive. Perhaps the kids can help me out with this…

In order to survive the woods, we need…(*Food, water, shelter*!)

Yes! The Holy Trinity of Survival! So anyway, on Day 1 the kids worked together to build an amazing shelter. We also met an important character from the Bible. A man named Job. Job was a man who loved God very much. But one day, Satan decided to test his faith by tormenting him. His goal was to turn Job away from God. Satan sent several obstacles and tragedies to Job's life, beginning with the killing several of his field workers and animal caretakers. Not only was this very sad, but it also meant that his farming business would suffer.

(To the children) But did Job turn away from God? (No.)

That's right. He knew that even when we are lost…*God leads the way!*

This reminds me, we also met someone else while out here in the woods.

(Gesture to kids) Do you know who else we met?   Rowdy Woods!

(Rowdy Woods enters)

Rowdy: (irritably) What is all this noise? Who is….oh, the rescue team! Well, as a matter of fact I *am* glad to see you. Now I can retreat back to my quiet and peaceful time alone!

Leader: Hi Rowdy! Yes, it appears that all these parents are here to rescue us from the woods. But first we have to tell them all about our week. (To parents) You see, Rowdy Woods is a hermit. He seems to have a bit in common with Job. Rowdy had a good job, and a successful career…until one day robots replaced his job. So he retreated to the woods and has been here ever since.

Rowdy: And it was perfectly peaceful until you all came along. But I have to say…you taught me a thing or two. For starters…that even when we are lost…*God leads the way!*

Lead students in song 1.

Leader: So on Day 2, we learned more about Job. Not only did Job suffer the loss of his workers, but also his children. He was so very sad. And he must have felt so anxious. But even when we are anxious…*God leads the way!*

Rowdy: I'm *not* afraid of the dark!

Leader: Um…no one said you were afraid of the dark…yet.

Rowdy: Oh! Of course. Well you know, what I meant to say is that I'm thankful you all taught me how to see how awesome our God is. Now I can look around at all the things he made and be *thankful* for it. Jesus is like a light in the darkness. Who needs a flashlight when you have Jesus?!

Lead kids in singing song 2.

Leader: On day 3 we met a really messy Beaver named Bobby. We learned Bobby's an amazing builder and swimmer. And although us humans can find Bobby and his friends rather frustrating at times because of the mess they make with trees, we learned that beavers are an important part of God's creation. It's easy for us to judge others about things we do not know. Even when things get messy…*God leads the way!*

That's right. We also learned that by day 3, we needed to find clean water to drink. So we spent a lot of time finding and cleaning water!

Lead kids in song 3:

Leader: This brings me back to Job. Job's friends came to visit him during his grieving. And they found Job to be sad and very confused. But even when we are confused…*God leads the way!* Right! So…now Job was sick and miserable with grief. Job's friends were at a bit of a loss on how to help him. So they tried to come up with lots of reasons why this might have happened to him…not knowing that Satan was behind it all. His own wife even went so far as to say "Curse God and die!" But instead of listening to such poor advice…Job loved God anyway! Eventually, Satan walked away from this situation, utterly defeated. In the end, God ended up blessing Job with a new family and a successful business once again.

So we learned a very important lesson from Job! That no matter what comes our way, to keep our eyes on God. Continue to pray, no matter how hard life gets!

Rowdy: And don't forget, even when we are confused…God leads the way!

Lead kids in song 4.

Leader: At the end of the week, we learned more about our savior Jesus. Long after the story of Job, God sent his only son to save us from our sins. Today we talked about the story of Jesus fishing with his friends. A storm suddenly approached and they were all very surprised. But they were even more surprised to see that Jesus was able to calm the storm with just a few words. So we learned that even when we are surprised…*God leads the way!!*

Speaking of storms, the kids learned a lot today about how to try to predict the weather without any electronics. So if you see them bird-watching, poking and prodding at pine cones, or looking at flowers a little more closely, just know that they are paying a little closer attention to God's voice in nature. Who knows, they might be able to tell you something new and surprising. And even when we are surprised…*God leads the way!*

Last song

Leader: Well, Rowdy, what do you say? Are you ready to go back home?

Rowdy: (glances around) Well, I sure do like it here. But you all have shown me that people aren't so bad. And…I don't have to be angry with the robots. Because I have Jesus! And I should give all my worries to Jesus.

Leader: I think you're really starting to catch on Rowdy!

Rowdy: But can we come back to camp?

Leader: Of course! And don't forget, even if we get lost….God Leads the Way!

Important: Each day during opening you will introduce a mascot. You can purchase stuffed animals for this or you can simply draw or print a picture.

DAY 1:

Even when we are lost...God leads the way!

Preparation: Have the daily mascot handy and sitting in the decorations so that the kids can easily spot it.

Tried and True Tip! : *You will be telling some fun facts about the animal mascot each day. A fun way to keep kids' attention as you do this, is by hiding the facts in Easter eggs or on post it notes and sticking them around the room. Call on different kids to retrieve a "fact egg" for you and bring it to you to read out loud to every one.*

Leader: Welcome to VBS! Are you all ready to learn about God and Jesus this week? Are you ready to dance and be silly and have the time of you life?! Yes!

Before we begin, I want to make sure we can hear our groups out here in the woods. The first group we have is the Lil' Hooties! If you're looking for a Lil Hootie, you may want to listen for some hooting sounds. Can the Lil' Hooties make some noise for me? (Encourage the group to make owl hooting sounds).

Okay, that's great! And I also know that we have Wolf Pack in the room. (Gesture to the wolf pack) Can the wolves make some noise?

Very good! And last, I know we have some bears in here! (Encourage group to make bear noises)

This is a great way to get everyone's attention when they are feeling especially rowdy. You'll definitely want to use it at the end of the night!

Say to the children: I am so glad that you all have decided to join me out here in this beautiful forest. Let's take a moment to admire the beautiful trees and all the things that nature has to offer. We have such an amazing Creator, who is our Father God in Heaven!

Does anyone here see any interesting animals nearby?

Yes, (pick up the owl) this is an owl! And you will never guess what his name is—it's Hootie! How many of you have heard an owl hoot? Yes, owls have a very unique sound when they decide to make a call.

Let's learn about owls!

• Owls are nocturnal—they hunt and play at night

- Owls are a predator bird, which means they hunt other small animals such as mice and even other owls!

- Owls can turn their heads almost completely around

- A group of owls is called a parliament

- Not all owls "hoot"! Some scream or whinny like a horse!

- Owls have an amazing ability to find things using their big eyes.

Say: It sure sounds like God made a very interesting creature. Owls are beautiful birds, and they are very smart. God gave them really big eyes and special wings to make it possible for them to search and hunt for food. They are very important to God's world! For example, they help keep disease in check by eliminating an overpopulation of rodents.

Okay, we have ONE more thing to do before we go today. I want everyone to close your eyes. Take a step to the right….to the left…ok turn around.

Without opening your eyes, can anyone tell me where North is? Shout it out!

(Listen to answers)

Oh no…it seems like…like we have lost our way! (Gasp dramatically).But wait…this is okay. Because we are together! And, we have Jesus! We have God! And even when we are lost… God Leads the Way!

Say it with me: God Leads the Way! Very good! Ok. Here's how this works. When I say "Even when we are lost" you *yell* "God Leads the Way!"

**Try this a few times and then release students to their stations.

If there is extra time, have the music teacher do one song with the kids.

DAY 2

Even when we are anxious...God Leads the way!

Call the children's attention by asking them to take turns making their group animal sounds.

Leader: Welcome back! We're here together again for another amazing day at VBS! Yesterday, we went off and got ourselves lost! But we learned that even when we are lost, (God leads the way!)

That's right. But I have to tell you, while I was getting ready for sleep in our shelter last night… I started to get a little worried. It was dark, there were so many new noises, and…I began to miss my family. I was feeling *anxious*. Have any of you ever felt *anxious* before? (Allow kids to offer answers).

Yes, it is totally normal for us to feel anxious sometimes. But today we are going to try our best to remember that even when we are anxious, God Leads the way! Let's try that again. Even when we are anxious…God leads the way!

Very good.

Now, you may have noticed that we have a new friend on set with us today. (Gesture to the stuffed rabbit that you placed on set earlier).

Yes, this is Jumpy the rabbit! There are many rabbits like jumpy in the woods! Have any of you ever met a real rabbit before? (Allow answers). You may have noticed that rabbits are very, well, jumpy! They are very nervous animals in general. That is because they are aware that they are prey animals. That means many predators like to hunt rabbits. Large birds, coyotes, wolves, and even house cats will hunt rabbits. So it's no wonder that Jumpy here is very *anxious*.

Let's take a moment to learn about God's beautiful creation—rabbits!

(Call on kids to help you retrieve rabbit facts)

- Rabbit teeth grow constantly! Because of what they eat, they are able to wear down their teeth.

- Rabbits cannot vomit . If they eat something that is bad for them, they'll have no other choice but to digest it!

- Female rabbits are called does, like a deer!

- Rabbits have eyes on the side of their head—this helps them see potential threats around them!

- Rabbits communicate by thumping.

- Rabbits show affection by licking

- Rabbits can be litter box trained, like a cat!

- Rabbits LOVE having lots of friends. It helps them feel safe!

God made rabbits special and unique! And Jumpy here is a good reminder that even when are anxious, God leads the way!

(Lead kids in a song, if there is time, and then release them to their stations).

DAY 3

Even when things get messy...God leads the way!

Call kids' attention by asking them to take turns with their animal group sounds.

Leader: Welcome back to day three of VBS! We have been lost in the woods for three days now! Has it been fun? So far this week we have met animals, we have built a shelter, and learned to build fire, we've met a hermit (Rowdy Woods) *and* we have had a blast! I have to say, if I have to be lost in the woods, I am glad it is with this crew because you all are so much fun!

And most of all, I am learning every day to lean a little more on God. As we continue to learn about Job and his story, we should remember to be thankful and follow Job's example and never give up on God. Even when we are lost...(God leads the way)...Or even when we are anxious....(God leads the way!) and today we will say this: Even when things get messy....God leads the way! Very good.

Now, why would things start to get "messy" when we are lost in the woods? (Allow kids to answer) Yes, very good. We might like to take a bath or find clean water for drinking by day three of our survival journey! Speaking of messy...does anyone see a new critter on set today? (Allow kids to spot the beaver).

This is Bobby the Beaver! And boy, let me tell you something about Bobby...he is rather messy! And when I first saw him, I thought what a messy little critter! But that wasn't a nice thing for me to think about a critter I don't know very much about!

(Call up volunteers to help you reveal beaver facts from Easter eggs or Post-It notes)

• Beavers are very hard workers! Beavers can cut down several trees in just a days time! They do this to build water dams, which redirects waterways in the wild. Many people do not like beavers because of this, but God made them this way so that beavers can help keep waterways cleaner and provide healthy habitats for other water dwelling animals!

• Beavers use their (orange) teeth to cut down entire trees!

• Like rabbits, beavers' teeth don't stop growing!

• When there is danger, beavers will slap the ground or water with their tail.

• Beavers are mostly nocturnal and tend to work and play most at night time

• Beavers can stay underwater for 6-8 minutes

Jena Robertson
Copyright 2023

Leader: God sure did make an amazing creature when he made beavers! Because they are always building and working, beavers can make quite a mess! And many people get frustrated with beavers because they are so messy! But it is important to understand that just because it looks messy to us, doesn't mean that it's not a part of God's incredible design! The beavers have important jobs in our world! And they have to make a mess to do it. Yes, they have to redirect waterways so that other water animals can live healthy lives!

Bobby the Beaver reminds us today that even when things get messy….God leads the way!

If there is time, have kids do a song and then release to class.

DAY 4

Call kids' attention by having their group take turns with animal sounds.

Leader: Welcome back to VBS! Wow, can you believe we've been stuck out here for four days? We have had quite an adventurous week! And we have learned so much about survival, God, and our friend Job. But I have to say trying to keep all this new stuff straight can get confusing.

But I have good news. Even when we are confused, God Leads the Way!

Does anyone see any new friends on our set today? (Allow kids to answer)

Yes! Today Skippy the Squirrel joins us! Everyone say, "Hi Skippy!" Skippy the squirrel is another amazing part of God's creation.

How many of you have ever been riding in the car, and seen a squirrel running across the road. Did they change their mind half way across? Did they go back and forth a bit and look a bit confused?

Yes! God gave squirrels this ability to zig zag quickly as a way to confuse and outrun predators. They may appear confused and forgetful at times, and that is also a special way that God made them!

Squirrels love to hoard acorns and nuts. They often bury an abundance of tree nuts in various places. They usually plan to come back in the winter to dig those things back up and eat them. But many times, squirrels become confused about where they buried their cache or they forget about some places altogether. And can you guess what happens then? Trees grow!

Yes, squirrels are very helpful planters and they play a huge role in helping God grow forests for our world! Even when we are confused…God leads the way!

Let's learn some more fun squirrel facts:

• Squirrels are the only mammals that can run really fast down a tree head first

• The presence of squirrels in a forest is a good indicator of how healthy a forest is. The more squirrels that are around, the healthier it is!

• Squirrels can be sneaky. If they think someone is watching them bury their nuts, they will pretend to dig a hole and hide them, only to put the nuts in its mouth and find somewhere else!

Day 5

Leader: Welcome back to VBS! It is our last day together here! Do you think someone will send a rescue team? Do you think we will find our way out?

Regardless of what happens, I know one thing for sure. I am glad we made it through this together! But our journey is not done here. Yesterday we finished up our story about Job. Today in Bible Adventures we will meet another very important person in the Bible!

Without telling you, I'll give you a clue. He helps us cope with big surprises!

Have any of you ever felt surprised before? (Allow answers)

Yes, sometimes being surprised is fun. But sometimes surprises can catch us off guard.

Have someone off stage make thunder sounds, either using a speaker or pots and pans.

(Gasp dramatically) Yes, sometimes thunderstorms can catch us off guard. That definitely isn't a pleasant surprise when you're lost in the woods! But even when we are surprised…God leads the way!

It's a good thing that you all prepared and built a shelter for us to stay dry in, just in case it rains.

Our new critter today is someone who is very serious about being prepared! It is Amy the Ant! (Have a child help retrieve Amy from the set and hand it to you).

Does anyone have any idea how an ant might help us know whether it's going to storm? (Allow guesses)

Ants are always working and preparing. They often prepare for oncoming rain by building their ant hills taller, to deter water from drowning them out.

Let's uncover some other fun facts about ants!

• Ants talk to each other using their antennas. Many times you will see them rubbing antennas and that is why!

• Most ants you see are female

• They are very strong! They can lift up to 50 times their own body mass!

• Ants are big believers in team work! There are many different jobs for ants and they work together to build things like bridges and homes. Not to mention they forage for food!

- In fact, ants work in shifts. That means they work for a while, then take a break to eat and sleep. During that time, other ants take over their work until they wake up!

- Ants have even been observed to yawn and stretch when they wake up!

Ants are very special creatures! They might be small, but they are intelligent and God created them that way! But we can learn something from ants—we should always be prepared. We want to prepare for storms. But most importantly, we want to prepare our hearts for Jesus. We can do that by asking for forgiveness for our sins, and working hard every day to serve others in a good way. That is a sure way to prepare ourselves for the amazing Kingdom of Heaven!

Lead kids in song, and release to classes.

Table of Contents

Please note: This curriculum is mostly organized by the day. All stations, crafts, activities and camp closing scripts will be found under the day for all stations. For ease of use, it is suggested to buy multiple copies of this book for your station leaders to use, but it is not necessary.

Made in United States
Cleveland, OH
28 May 2025

17291330R00046